Rationalism

By
J. M. Robertson

RATIONALISM
1. THE TERM

The names 'rationalist' and 'rationalism' have been used in so many senses within the past three hundred years that they cannot be said to stand quite definitely for any type or school of philosophic thought. For Bacon, a 'rationalist' or rationalis was a physician with a priori views of disease and bodily function; and the Aristotelian humanists of the Helmstadt school were named rationalistas about the same period by their opponents. A little later some Continental scholars applied the name to the Socinians and deists; and later still it designated, in Britain, types of Christian thinkers who sought to give a relatively reasoned form to articles of the current creed which had generally been propounded as mysteries to be taken on faith. The claim to apply 'reason' in such matters was by many orthodox persons regarded as in itself impious, while others derided the adoption of the title of 'rationalist' or 'reasonist' by professing Christians as an unwarranted pretence of superior reasonableness. Used in ethics, the label 'rationalism' served in the earlier part of the eighteenth century to stigmatise, as lacking in evangelical faith, those Christians who sought to make their moral philosophy quadrate with that of 'natural religion.' Later in the century, though in England we find the status of 'rational' claimed for orthodox belief in miracles and prophecies as the only valid evidence for Christianity, rationalism became the recognised name for the critical methods of the liberal German theologians who sought to reduce the supernatural episodes of the Scriptures to the status of natural events misunderstood; and several professed histories of modern 'rationalism' have accordingly dealt mainly or wholly with the developments of Biblical criticism in Germany.

New connotations, however, began to accrue to the terms in virtue of the philosophical procedure of Kant's Critique of Pure Reason, though hisReligion within the Bounds of Simple [blossen] Reason went far to countenance the current usage; and when Hegel subsequently proceeded to identify (at times) reason with the cosmic process, there were set up implications which still give various technical significances to 'rationalism' in some academic circles. In the brilliant work of Professor William James on Pragmatism, for instance, the term is represented as connoting, in contrast to the thinking of 'tough-minded' empiricists, that of a type or school of 'tender-minded' people who are collectively —

'Rationalistic (going by "principles")

Intellectualistic

Idealistic

Optimistic

Religious

Free-willist

Monistic

Dogmatical.'

Yet it is safe to say that in Britain, for a generation back, the name has carried to the general mind only two or three of the connotations in Professor James's list, and much more nearly coincides with his contrary list characterising 'the tough-minded':—

'Empiricist (going by "facts")

Sensationalistic

Materialistic

Pessimistic

Irreligious

Fatalistic

Pluralistic

Skeptical'

— though here again the item 'pluralistic' does not chime with the common conception, and 'pessimistic' is hardly less open to challenge. 'Intellectualistic' appears to be aimed at Hegelians, but would be understood by many as describing the tendency to set up 'reason' against 'authority'; and Professor James's 'rationalists,' who would appear to include thinkers like his colleague Professor Royce, would not be so described in England by many university men, clergymen, or journalists. The name 'rationalist,' in short, has come to mean for most people in this country very much what 'freethinker' used to mean for those who did not employ it as a mere term of abuse. It stands, that is to say, for one who rejects the claims of 'revelation,' the idea of a personal God, the belief in personal immortality, and in general the conceptions logically accruing to the practices of prayer and worship.

Perhaps the best name for such persons would be 'naturalist,' which was already in use with some such force in the time of Bodin and Montaigne. Kant, it may be remembered, distinguished between 'rationalists,' as thinkers who did not deny the possibility of a revelation, and 'naturalists' who did. But though 'naturalism,' has latterly been recognised by many as a highly convenient term for the view of things which rejects 'supernaturalism,' and will be so used in the present discussion, the correlative 'naturalist' has never, so to speak, been naturalised in English. For one thing, it has been specialised in ordinary language in the sense of 'student of nature,' or rather of what has come to be specially known as 'natural history'—in particular, the life of birds, insects, fishes, and animals. And, further, the term 'naturalism,' like every other general label for a way of thinking, is liable to divagations and misunderstandings. Some thinkers (known to the present writer only through the accounts given of them by others) appear to formulate as a philosophic principle the doctrine that the best way to regulate our lives is to find out how the broad processes of 'Nature' is tending, and to conform to it alike our ideals and our practice. The notion is that if, say, Nature appears to be making for the extermination of backward races, we should try to help the process forward. It is doubtful whether more than a very small number of instructed men have ever entertained such a principle. It is certainly not the expression of the philosophy of those ancients who sought to 'live according to Nature'; and it would certainly not have been assented to by such modern 'naturalists' as Spencer and Huxley and Mill. But if the principle is current at all, it makes the name of 'naturalist' as ambiguous philosophically as 'rationalist' can be.

And similar drawbacks attach to another set of terms which have much to recommend them—'positive,' 'positivist,' and 'positivism.' They stand theoretically for (1) the provable, (2) the attitude of the seeker for intelligible proof in all things, (3) the conviction that the rights of reason are ultimate and indefeasible. But here again, to say nothing of the equivoque of 'positive,' we are met by a claim of pre-emption, the claim of Comte to associate the 'ism' specifically with his system, theoretic and practical. And for the majority of men with positivist proclivities, the gist of the 'practical application' of Comte is incompatible with the positive spirit. Positivism with a capital P is thereby made for them, as it was for Littré, something alien to positivism as the free scientific spirit would seek to shape it. And a wrangle over the ownership of the word would be a waste of time.

2. THE PRACTICAL POSITION

The usages being so, most of us who can answer to the term 'rationalist' may reasonably let its general force be decided for us by the stream of tendency in ordinary speech; and, recognising the existence of other applications, one may usefully seek to give a philosophic account of what its adoption seems to involve. That is to say, the present treatise does not undertake to present, much less to justify, all the views which have ever been described as 'rationalistic,' but merely to present current rationalism in the broad sense indicated, as on the one hand an outcome of tendencies seen at work in the earlier movements so named, and on the other hand as apparently committing its representatives to a certain body or class of conclusions. For there is this capital element in common for all the stirrings known by the name of rationalism, that they stand for 'private judgment' as against mere tradition or mere authority. Early 'rationalists' might indeed seek to put a quasi-rational form upon tradition, and to give reasons for recognising authority. But in their day and degree they had their active part in the evolution of the critical faculty, inasmuch as they outwent the line of mere acquiescence; and views which to-day form part of uncritically accepted creeds were once products of innovating (however fallacious) reasoning. There is no saltum mortale in the evolution of thought. The very opponents of the rationalist often claim to be more rational than he, and must at least use his methods up to a certain point. This is done even by the quasi-skeptical school, of whom some claim to subordinate reason to some species of insight which they either omit to discriminate intelligibly from the process of judgment, or do not admit to need its sanction.

'Rationalism,' then, is to be understood relatively. To be significant to-day, accordingly, it should stand first and last for the habit and tendency to challenge the doctrines which claim 'religious' or sacrosanct authority—to seek by reflection a defensible theory of things rather than accept enrolment under traditional creeds which demand allegiance on supernaturalist grounds.

Of such thinkers the number is daily increasing. There are now, probably, tens of thousands of more or less instructed men and women in this country who would call themselves rationalists in the broad sense above specified as now generally current. They are all, probably, Darwinians orevolutionists, mostly 'monists' in Spencer's way, 'determinists' in the philosophic sense of that term if they have worked at the 'free-will' problem at all, and non-believers in personal immortality. Very few, at least, bracket the term 'rationalist' with 'spiritualist' in describing themselves: the two tendencies nearly always divide sharply, though it cannot be said that in strict logic they are mutually exclusive. Of most, the philosophic attitude approximates broadly to that of Spencer, though many recognise and avow the inexpertness of Spencer's metaphysic. Only a few, probably, if any, could properly be termed 'skeptics' in the strict philosophic sense of doubters of all inferences. That is a mental attitude more often professed by defenders of 'revelation,' as Pascal and Huet, who seek to make the judgment despair of itself in preparation for an act of assent which is already discredited by such despair. Yet it belongs to the rationalistic attitude to be ready, in consistency, to analyse all one's own convictions and listen candidly to all negations of them. A belief in the possibility of rational certitude is implicit in every process of sincere criticism; but the discrimination or gradation of certitudes is the task of rational philosophy.

As we shall see, quasi-rational certitude as regards the process of evolution is challenged from two points of view by professed believers in the reality of that process. One school argues that scientific conclusions are all uncertain because the ultimate assumptions of science are unverifiable, and that, accordingly, religious assumptions, being neither more nor less rational than others, may 'reasonably' stand. Others argue that the process of judgment or reasoning which is held to establish scientific truth is not adequate to any theory of interpretation; and that, accordingly, some species of divination—which in the terms of the case eludes judgment—is to be relied on. Such thinkers ostensibly profess to 'reason' to the effect that reasoning is invalid. Against them, those who claim to hold by reason as the totality of judgment may fitly call themselves by the name 'rationalist.'

Given such a general attitude, then, to what philosophic form is it justifiably to be reduced? Those who have longest meditated the question will perhaps be the least quick to give a precise and confident answer. If training in the scrupulous use of reason sets up any mental habit in face of large problems, it is the habit of tentative approach; and the rationalist of to-day should be a much less readily self-satisfied thinker than the former claimants to the name. Professor James, indeed, is able to reconcile an ostensible certainty of rightness of method and result with much experience in investigation. 'A pragmatist,' he tells us, 'turns his back resolutely and once for all upon a lot of inveterate habits dear to professional philosophers. He turns away from abstraction and insufficiency, from verbal solutions, from fixed principles, closed systems, and pretended absolutes and origins.' One is delighted to hear it; but it is perhaps the course of prudence for most of us to doubt our power of getting entirely clear of inveterate habits. Scrutiny of philosophic literature fails to reveal any one who entirely succeeded in it, even slowly. A constant concern for revision, then, would seem to be forced upon the professed rationalist, who knows how often the appeal to reason has yielded mere modifications of error, one unjustifiable credence ousting another. 'Knows,' one says, because the error is provable to the satisfaction of the judgment which seeks certainty. Such negative knowledge is the promise of positive.

3. THE RELIGIOUS CHALLENGE

It is fitting, then, at the very outset to make a critical scrutiny of the implications of our term. Rationalism, broadly, implies the habitual resort to reason, to reflection, to judgment. The rationalist, in effect, says, 'That which I find to be incredible I must disbelieve, whatever prestige may attach to its assertion; that which I find to be doubtful or inconceivable I will so describe. Finding the practice of prayer to be incompatible not only with any sincere belief in natural law, but with the professed religious beliefs of the more educated of those who resort to it, I will not pray. Seeing all religions to be but halting manipulations of the guesses and intuitions of savages, to be still as uncritically credulous in their affirmations as they are blind in their denials, and to be thus mere loose modifications of older beliefs felt to be astray, I will go behind them all for my own theory of things, getting all the help I can alike from those who have reasoned most loyally on the deeper problems involved, and from those who have striven mostcircumspectly to understand the process of causation in the universe.'

So far, the procedure is one of rejecting demonstrably fallacious beliefs in regard to the general order of things, substantially on the lines on which tested and testable conclusions have been substituted for old delusions in what we term 'the sciences.' At every step the rationalist is assailed, just as were and are the reformers of the sciences; first by angry epithets, then by bad arguments as to 'evidence,' then by cooler attempts to demonstrate that his method will lead to moral harm, whether or not to present or future punishment at the hands of an angry God. In particular he is assured that on his principles there can be no restraint upon men's evil proclivities; and that even the most thoughtful man runs endless dangers of wrong-doing when he substitutes his private judgment for the 'categorical imperative' embodied either in religious codes or in the current body of morality. To such representations the critical answer is that undoubtedly the application of reason to moral issues incurs the risks of fallacy which beset all reasoning in science so-called; but that, on the other hand, every one of those risks attaches at least equally to all acceptance of 'authoritative' teaching. Galileo could not well err worse than ancient Semites or Christian priests in matters scientific; and Clifford could not conceivably div agate more dangerously in morals than did the plotters and agents of the Massacre of St. Bartholomew. Even if we put out of the account the overwhelming record of undenied wickedness wrought in the name of God and faith, there never has been, and there is no prospect of our ever seeing, unanimity of moral opinion among even the most disciplined types of religious believers in 'authority.' Even in the Catholic Church it would be difficult to find any two men of judicial habit of mind who agree in all points as to what is 'right.'

Nor is the rationalist's position a whit more open to utilitarian criticism (for his religious opponents, it will be observed, are narrowly utilitarian even in professing to combat his utilitarianism) when he is challenged upon his acceptance of 'the voice of conscience,' otherwise the 'categorical imperative.' The Kantian argument on that head is a fallacy of shifting terms. Mental hesitation as to obeying the sense of 'ought' is the proof of the vacillation of the perception of 'oughtness.' When I feel, first, that I 'ought' to forgive a peculator, and then that I 'ought' to give him up to 'justice'; or, alternatively, that I ought to rise earlier, and, again, that I may as well enjoy more sleep, I have reduced the 'categorical imperative' to the last term in a calculation. And exactly the same thing is done by the believer who is perplexed as to the 'voice of God.' Religious history and biography are full of avowals, on the one hand, of the murderous clash of convictions alike resting on 'revelation' of all kinds, and, on the other hand, of the agonies of zealots 'wrestling in prayer' to know what is really the divine will. Cromwell's life illustrates both orders of dilemma, with a sufficiency of resultant moral evil to arrest propaganda on the side of faith. And the philosopher of the 'categorical imperative' miscarries as instructively as does the soldier of divine will. Kant, on the one hand, vetoes even the telling of a lie to a would-be murderer to put him astray, and, on the other hand, commends to 'enlightened' clergymen the systematic preaching of their religion in a double sense, because populus vult decipi. The 'categorical imperative,' as propounded by him, is a form of self-deception.

When, again, the psychic facts are critically faced and the 'categorical imperative' is rationally recognised as either the sum of the persisting moral judgments or the mere verbalism that we ought to do what we feel we ought to do, the rationalist is still at no disadvantage, utilitarian or other. It is not there that his tether tightens. Religious morality, as finally ratified by the more thoughtful among religious men, is but the endorsement of 'natural' morality. There is not one social commandment, as distinguished from religious or ritualist dogma, that did not emerge as a prescription of the natural moral sense, primitive or otherwise—a supererogatory proof that the religious prescriptions are from the same source. All surviving religious ethic is to-day actually accredited as such, precisely because—and only in so far as—it conforms to natural judgment. Without resort to that tribunal, the religionist could not discriminate between the sanction of the sixth commandment and the law of the levirate, which he has cancelled.

The religious sanction, therefore, is logically null, in terms of the religious man's own mental processes. There is left him, to discredit the rationalist, only the threat that the God whom he terms infinitely good will or may punish the unbeliever for not believing on the strength of a Bible packed with incredible narrative and indefensible doctrine. The anti-rationalist position is thus reduced to 'Pascal's wager'—at once the most childish and, from the standpoint of other and nobler religious thought, the most irreligious argument ever advanced by a competent intelligence on the side of faith. Pascal's thesis is that if the unbeliever is wrong, he runs a frightful risk of future torment; whereas, if he should after all be right, he will be no worse off after death for having believed. So the 'belief' required of him is a simple mindless and faithless conformity to a conditional threat. To such moral perversity can religion persuade.

To Pascal's wager there have been many retorts. Mill declared that if a God should doom him to hell for having been unable to believe in such a God, 'to hell he would go'—glad, by implication, not to be in heaven. Mansel's sole answer was a puerile attempt at a pious sneer. Clifford, in effect, denounced the Pascalian appeal for what it was, a base appeal to fear. But it is unnecessary to resort to such logical supererogation. There are two obvious and decisive rebuttals to Pascal's doctrine on purely logical ground. Firstly, his thesis is available to the Moslem or the polytheist no less than to the Christian; and when put from either of these sides it leaves the Christian running the very risk with which he menaces the unbeliever. He may have chosen the wrong God. Secondly, the hypothetical Good God, if in any intelligible sense worthy of the name, would conceivably be as likely to send Pascal to hell for dishonouring him as to send the honest atheist there for refusing to make-believe. The pietist has dishonoured himself to no purpose.

The a posteriori argument for religious conformity has thus come to nothing; and the process of argument has revealed the religio-utilitarian champion of morality as traitor to that cause. There is left him, indeed, the plea that religious fears and sanctions are good for the ill-disposed believer, who ought, therefore, not to be disillusioned. As regards the simple dogma of deity, the position has the emphatic support of Voltaire. But Voltaire declined to use the favourite menaces of faith, as do many religionists of to-day; and if those menaces are to be rationally vindicated, there must first be raised the question whether they could not be improved upon for the purpose professed. Leaving that task to those who affect them, the rationalist may claim to be justified in acting on the maxim that honesty is the best policy in the intellectual as in the commercial life. There has been no such historical harvest of moral betterment from the religion of fear as could induce him of all men to employ it as a moral prophylactic.

Thus far he figures as the vindicator of simple veracity against those who, in the name of morals, would make it of no account. He has still to meet, indeed, the challenge: What of the ill-disposed among your own way of thinking? If an unbeliever should see his way to gain by falsehood or licit fraud, what should deter him? Much satisfaction appears to be derived by many well-meaning people from the propounding of this dilemma. They may or may not be gratified by the answer that if a rationalist should not be, by training and bias, spontaneously averse to lying and cheating, or generally unwilling to do otherwise than he would be done by, or sensitive enough to the blame of his fellows to fear it, there is indeed no more security for his veracity or honesty than for that of a typical Jesuit or a pious company promoter. One can but add that, seeing that in the terms of the case he began by unprofitably avowing an unpopular opinion, he is presumably, on the average, rather less likely to lie for gain than those who confessedly find the sheer fear of consequences a highly important consideration in their own plan of life, and who have at the same time the promise from their own code of plenary pardon for all sins on the simple condition of ultimate repentance.

4. THE PHILOSOPHICAL CHALLENGE

But we have now clearly imported into the rationalist philosophy a principle or factor which ostensibly rivals or primes reason. The rationalist avows a moral bias—an attitude towards his fellows, a moral 'taste,' let us say—which partly determines his reasoned judgment. He has a conception of goodness in virtue of which he finds 'revelation' frequently repellent and the popular 'God' a chimera; even as the believer finds them satisfactory because they are in part conformable to his moral and speculative bias, and he has been brought up to pretermit judgment beyond those limits. This bias appears to be partly congenital, partly acquired; though most men are agreed that many who reveal a given bias would have presented another had they been differently trained. Certain forms of congenital bias, that is to say, yield more or less easily to others, specially fostered or exercised. Whatever be the respective force of the generative factors, the fact of bias remains; and there is no escape from the conclusion that it operates in regard to 'intellectual' as well as to 'moral' judgments—to judgments, that is, of causal interpretation or non-moral discrimination as well as to judgments upon human action.

The rationalist, in fact, is merely a person who in certain directions carries the processes of doubt, analysis, and judgment further than do persons of a different habit of mind. His neighbour, who believes in 'God' or 'the saints' or Mrs. Eddy, may chance to carry those processes in other directions further than he,—may be more reflective and experimental and judicious, for instance, in matters of diet,—may even be an analytical thinker in matters of science to which the so-called rationalist has given no independent thought. There are well-known instances of men of science who by analysis widen the bounds of physical knowledge while accepting, in ways which other men find grotesquely uncritical, loose propositions on psychic existence. When sounds are heard from furniture, the rationalist, with his naturalistic bias, looks for explanations in terms of physics; while the spiritualist, even if he chance to be a professed physicist, looks for them in terms of speculative psychics.

Upon a strictly impartial and 'objective' consideration, the two kinds of bias are seen to be alike forms of craving, desires seeking satisfaction. Both inquirers seek for 'causes.' But one has the habit of seeking causes in terms of sequences of known or intelligible processes, capable of willed repetition; the other yearns to find proof of the existence of non-material personalities in the cosmos and in his personal neighbourhood, and, believing in such existence in advance, either provisionally or rootedly, hopes to bring others to his way of thinking by a demonstration that certain physical phenomena are not physically producible. And it must be granted him that herein he is theoretically at par with the man of science — physical or moral — who, having spontaneously framed a hypothesis, seeks to find that facts conform to it. Every man with a hypothesis, broadly speaking, wants to find that facts are so-and-so.

The rationalist, then, has his bias like another. Though it takes in part a critical or negative form, it is fundamentally as positive as another. He has come to crave for coherence and consistency in narratives, statements, explanations, arguments, propositions, and systems of thought; even as his 'contrary' or competitor has come to crave for evidence that something 'supernatural' wields a purposive and 'intelligent' control, mediate or immediate, over all things, using among others 'supernormal' means. This 'contrary' thinker may or may not believe in 'spirits' in the ordinary sense, may or may not believe in the immortality of human minds; but if he is really to be an opponent of the rationalist bias he is to be classed as having a bias to traditional or authoritative views of the cosmos, to religious as against naturalistic explanations of history, to a conception of the human as of the extra-human processes in terms of a controlling will and purpose. He too, it is true, must have some craving for coherence and consistency — else he could not debate and reason at all; but the other craving in him has primed that.

It is a fallacy, we may note in passing, to suppose that the 'agnostic' attitude, so-called, is something between the two main forms of bias here posited. Agnosticism, logically carried out, can differentiate from other forms of rationalism only in local limitation of belief; and in practice it is not often found to do even that. The agnostic inevitably begins in terms of the rationalist bias, in craving for coherence and consistency of statement; and his most circumspect negations stand for precaution against inconsistent credulity. But precisely in virtue of that bias, he is the opponent of the supernaturalist bias. He does not in effect merely say, 'I do not know': he implicitly says 'You do not know' to the professor of non-natural knowledge.

Bias, then, being clearly posited, the debate at once turns—as indeed it usually does even without formal acknowledgment of bias—to a competition of claims to consistency. All debate presupposes agreement on something. As antagonists in religion appeal either to God-idea or to Bible, to probability or to usage, to expediency or to authority, or to historic evidence for one revelation as against another, so antagonists upon the fundamentals of religion appeal to accepted laws of proof, measures of evidence, consistency of reasoning. The most tenacious of traditionists must put his case in a 'reasoned' form. And therein, of course, lies the secret of the gradual historic dissolution of traditional credence in the minds of those who come at all within the range of the argument. Every act of reasoning—as priesthoods are more or less clearly aware—is a concession to the rationalist position to begin with; and only superior skill in fence can ostensibly countervail the advantage thus given to the disputant who claims that reason must determine beliefs. Reasoning against the validity of reason is recognisable as suicidal by all who can reason coherently. If reason be untrustworthy, what is the value of reasoning to that effect? Either you go by reason or you do not. If not, you are out of the debate, or you are grasping your sword by the blade, a course not long to be persisted in. Even the skeptical defender of religion, following religious precedent, says, 'Come now, let us reason together.'

Thus we reach the standing anomaly that the defence of faith against rationalistic criticism alternately takes the courses of pronouncing the appeal to reason a foolish presumption, and of claiming to reason more faithfully than the rationalist. The two positions being, to say the least, incompatible from the point of view of dialectic, we must fight upon one or the other at a time; and, having briefly dealt with the former, we may fitly consider at greater length the latter. The more philosophic assailant of the rationalist, we assume, professes after all to stand or fall by reasoning. That is to say, he claims to hold his supernaturalist positions in logical and moral consistency with his historical positions, his practice as a judge or juror, as a man of science, as a critic in politics, as a man of honour, as a player of cricket by the rules of the game. As a matter of fact, however, he at times goes about the task by way of an undertaking to show, not that his beliefs are well founded in reason, but that no beliefs are; and that his beliefs are therefore at least as valid as any one else's. All the while he is ostensibly appealing to reason, to judgment. That position in turn must be considered.

5. THE SKEPTICAL RELIGIOUS CHALLENGE

The philosophic issue under this head has been usefully cleared for English readers by Mr. A. J. Balfour in his Defence of Philosophic Doubt; and, in another sense, very usefully for rationalists by the same writer in his work The Foundations of Belief. The gist of the former treatise is an expansion of the proposition of Hume that all moral judgments, on analysis, are found to root in a sentiment or bias. In particular, Mr. Balfour argues that all scientific beliefs so-called, however immediately proved, rest upon general beliefs which are 'incapable of proof.' It is noteworthy that never through the whole treatise does Mr. Balfour analyse the concept of 'proof,' though his main aim is ostensibly to discriminate between proved and unproved propositions. It may be worth while, then, at this stage, to note the risks of intellectual confusion in connection with the term proof. The common conception, implicit in Mr. Balfour's argument, is that concerning a 'proved' thing either we have, or men of science say we have, a right of certainty, as it were, which we cannot have concerning anything not proved or not capable of proof. The simple fact is that the very idea of proof involves that of uncertainty you seek to prove that which is not unquestionable. To prove is to probe, to test. The idea of 'demonstration,' which seems commonly to connote special certainty, carries us no further. It means a 'showing,' a 'letting you see with your own eyes.' In geometry, it stands for a chain of reasoning in which every step rests upon previous steps which ultimately rest upon axioms and definitions agreed upon. There the process is one of analysis—a showing that a proposition formerly unknown as such is really contained in or implied by propositions known. Certainty follows. Yet there is abundant record of 'proofs' or 'tests' which were fallacious, and of ostensible demonstrations which were flawed—modes of squaring the circle, for instance. The ultimate in the matter is the belief arrived at or evoked; and the significant fact for us is, that beliefs ostensibly so arrived at may be false, because the cited proof or evidence is erroneous or the demonstration inconsequent.

Certainty, on the other hand, attaches in the highest degree to certain beliefs that, in the nature of the case, are 'incapable of proof,' that is, of being tested. No belief is more certain for all men than the belief that they will all die, though the event, posited as future, cannot as such be 'tested.' In this case, the connotation of the word 'proof,' nevertheless, is by common consent transferred to the concept of mortality: the invariable dying of all previous men is allowed to be 'proof,' or decisive evidence, that all living men will die to the last generation. In regard to some other certainties, the concept of 'proof' is wholly irrelevant. You cannot 'prove' that you feel a pain, though it is one of the most certain of all facts for you while it lasts. If, then, any general scientific or other belief be shown to be 'incapable of proof,' in this merely negative sense (as distinguished from 'capable of disproof'), that is no argument against it for any practical or philosophic purpose. Such a belief is that in the 'uniformity of nature,' which is held by the same tenure as that in the mortality of all men. It cannot be 'proved,' either as to the past or the future, in the sense of being tested, save as regards past particulars, which are necessarily a small selection from the totality of phenomena. For the future, in the terms of the case, there can be no proof. Yet no man has any more doubt as to the rising of the sun to-morrow than as to his own ultimate death. Concerning this we are quite certain, which we cannot be as to many things reasonably held to have been 'proved.' Such and such are our 'certainties.'

What, then, is Mr. Balfour's case against men of 'science,' and those whom he calls 'the Freethinkers'? It may be put under three heads.

1. They are lax, he thinks, in their conception of proof. As it happens, he argues against Mill's criticism of the syllogism, which is that there can be no real inference from the premisses of a syllogism, because in the major premiss there is already asserted what is afterwards asserted in the conclusion. Mr. Balfour's reply is, that 'So long as in fact we do assert the major premiss without first believing the conclusion, so long will the latter be an inference from the former.' Now, Mill's express contention is that we never do assert the major premiss without first believing the conclusion; and the dispute resolves itself into one as to the proper meaning of 'inference.' Mill is at this point guarding against erroneous conceptions of proof; his thesis being that the 'proof' of the conclusion is not given in the

major, but in the body of evidence on which that is founded, and which carries the conclusion at the same time. As the kind of syllogism in question is the old one about the mortality of Sokrates, Mill here takes as 'proof' the evidence which all men now reckon sufficient to establish the fact of universal human mortality, though, as aforesaid, it is not literally a complete 'proof' at all. Mr. Balfour is arguing, if anything relevant to his main thesis, that a so-called 'inference' which is merely a statement in one particular of what is believed of all such particulars, is a 'real' inference, and therefore somehow more valid than inferences not so drawn. Perhaps he does not mean this: if so, the argument has no bearing on his main case.

Concerning 'inference,' the proper development of Mill's position would be that the processes of reasoning properly to be so called are either hypotheses still to be tested or beliefs held by the tenure of uncontradicted experience. And inferences of the latter kind are in fact of the most various degrees of certainty. We 'infer' that we shall all die, not from the generalisation that all men are mortal, but from the accepted fact that all men hitherto have been. The major premiss in the typical syllogism is itself the inference. But we also infer, from a much narrower experience, that inasmuch as pitchblende, say, has been found to yield radium in certain very small quantities, other pitchblende will do so in future. Here the certainty is distinctly less: few men would wager heavily on it. And we may at once grant to Mr. Balfour that in this and many other cases 'scientific beliefs' fall far short of 'certainty,' as that term is established for us by other beliefs. As Mill put it, inference from particulars never can be formally cogent. He might have added as aforesaid, that all real inference as to events is from particulars, and that formal cogency belongs only to mathematics. Mr. Balfour says he will not 'go so far' as Mill. So that, whatever be Mill's inconsistencies—and they are many—Mill was at this point somewhat less confident of belief than Mr. Balfour.

2. Mr. Balfour impugns what he takes to be 'the most ordinary view of scientific philosophy, ... that science, in so far as it consists of a statement of the laws of phenomena, is founded entirely on observation and experiment,' which 'furnish not only the occasions of scientific discovery,

but also the sole evidence of scientific truth—evidence, however, which is considered by most men of science not only amply sufficient, but also as good as any which can be well imagined.' In this statement there are obvious laxities, which may serve as openings for idle dispute. No man of science, surely, holds that all statements of the laws of phenomena are equally well 'proved' by observation and experiment. They do hold that such a proposition as that of 'the uniformity of nature,' considered as a 'law of phenomena,' is founded on observation and experiment, as fully as any proposition of natural mode can be. But there is obvious room for ambiguity, again, in the expression 'laws of phenomena.' Let us consider, for instance,

3. Mr. Balfour's contention that the 'law of universal causation' is incapable of proof, and cannot properly be said to be founded on observation and experiment. Here the rationalist may safely grant him his whole case—at least the present writer does. He is right, I submit, in his criticism of Mill's ostensible attempt to prove that the so-called 'law of universal causation' is deduced from observation and experiment. I will further waive the question whether he rebuts the proof offered by Kant for his proposition that 'the judgment of sequence cannot be made without the presupposition of the judgment of causality,' which, like many of Kant's formulas, seems to me very awkwardly phrased. But I advance without hesitation the proposition that all reflection upon events involves the conception of universal causation, and that all reflection upon things involves the conception of them in eventu. And this necessary assumption is not as such a product of observation and experiment, though we can never exactly say how far experience may condition our manner of making the assumption. It is quite needless to trace the history of it in human experience, for it is clearly pre-human. If from a tree you fire at and wound a tiger who sees you, he will try to get at you, plainly regarding you as the cause of his wound, though he may never have been shot or seen a shot fired before. The accuracy of his inference is worth noting, though he might chance, of course, to have been wounded by a shot fired by an unseen companion of yours. It may 'reasonably' be 'inferred' (to use terms which Mr. Balfour would probably censure), that man has always obeyed the law of thought

thus illustrated; and no number of wrong particular inferences can affect the inevitableness of his assumption that any event has a cause. The concept of cause roots in primary animal habit.

Is this assumption, then, a 'law of phenomena' in Mr. Balfour's sense? is it to be ruled out, on his principles, as not being founded on observation and experiment? and are men of science thereby shown to be wrong in holding that every scientific statement of the laws of phenomena is so founded? I do not see how he can thus argue; for he has expressly contended (p. 135), that 'A law of nature refers to a fixed relation, not between the totality of phenomena, but between extremely small portions of that totality.' Is a law of phenomena, then, something other than a law of nature? This he cannot mean; and the conclusion is that the so-called 'law of universal causation' is not properly to be called a law of nature, or a law at all, unless we are so to call a necessary element of all reflection upon nature.

The dispute here, in short, resolves itself into a question of terminology; and it is quite likely that many men of science, and many freethinkers, have used lax terminology. But as regards the reasonableness of their beliefs, or their way of believing, in contrast with those of the supernaturalists whom Mr. Balfour champions, he has thus far made out no hostile case whatever. And when we come to what appear to be his conclusions, they are such as can wring no rationalist's withers. Our ultimate premisses, he contends, are incapable of proof. Granted—if the assumption of universal causation is to be termed a premiss, as is that of the uniformity of nature. The practical issue for him appears to be contained in this passage (italics ours):—

'That men ought not to give up on speculative grounds the belief in "the uniformity of nature, or any other great principle," I hold, as the reader will see if his patience lasts to the end of the volume, with as much persistence as any man. But I must altogether take exception to the statement, which is the central point of the argument just stated, namely, that the fact that these principles work in practice is any ground for believing them to be even approximately true' (p. 145).

Our patience may easily stand the suggested test, since Mr. Balfour's book is for the most part extremely well written; and unless I have totally misunderstood him, his conclusions are (a) that he and we do well to accept the general body of accepted scientific doctrines, including those of the theory of evolution and the uniformity of nature, without any ground for believing them to be even approximately true; and (b) that he and his co-believers do equally well to hold what he vaguely indicates (p. 324) as 'the Theological opinions to which I adhere,' also without 'any ground for believing them to be even approximately true.' In a sentence (p. 320) of which the diction is noticeably lax, he says: —

'...I and an indefinite number of other persons, if we contemplate Religion and Science as unproved systems of belief standing side by side, feel a practical need for both; and if this need is, in the case of those few and fragmentary scientific truths by which we regulate our animal actions, or an especially imperious and indestructible character — on the other hand, the need for religious truth, rooted as it is in the loftiest region of our moral nature, is one from which we would not, if we could, be freed.... We are in this matter,' he adds, 'unfortunately altogether outside the sphere of Reason.'

6. THE MEANING OF REASON

The problem as to 'the sphere of Reason' could not be more effectually raised. Mr. Balfour clearly implies that there is a sphere of Reason, but forces a perplexed query as to when he believes himself to enter it. Evidently, by his own definitions, his whole political life is lived outside it. Alike his generalisations from past history, and his predictions of the future, are such as afford 'no ground for believing them to be even approximately true': those of his opponents, of course, coming for him under the same category. He would, perhaps, hold himself to be in the sphere of Reason when following a proposition in mathematics; but he does not admit himself to be there even when he consents to believe that he will die, and that he had better avoid prussic acid. 'No experience, however large,' he insists (p. 75), 'and no experiments, however well contrived and successful, could give us any reasonable assurance that the co-existences or sequences which have been observed among phenomena will be repeated in the future.' Not 'certainty,' be it observed, but 'any reasonable assurance.' That is to say, we have no reasonable assurance that we shall die.

Obviously the extravagance of this proposition is calculated. The point is that no belief whatever concerning life and death and morality and the process of nature can be justified by 'reason'; and that accordingly no religious belief whatever can be discredited on the score of being opposed to reason or 'unreasonable.' If not more reasonable than the most carefully tested or the most widely accepted belief in science, or the belief that the sun will rise or fire burn to-morrow, or that we shall all die, it is not less reasonable than they. Therefore, believe as your bias leads.

It is only fair to Mr. Balfour to say that there is nothing new in his position, though probably it has never before been quite so violently formulated. The Greek Pyrrho (fl. 300-350) argued that almost all propositions were doubtful; and some of his followers are said to have been consistent enough to doubt whether they doubted. In the dialogues of Cicero we find the skeptical method employed, with supreme inconsistency, by the official exponents of unbelieved doctrines, to discredit competing doctrines.

Among the pagans it was also turned, with no special religious purpose, against all forms of dogmatic doctrine by Sextus the Empiric (fl. 200-250); and in the early Christian dialogue of Minucius Felix a pagan is presented as turning it against Christianity. In the later Middle Ages it is resorted to by Cornelius Agrippa, previously a great propounder of fantastic propositions in science, against the current science of his time, and in favour of a return to the simplicity of the early Christian creed. Still later, it was much resorted to, after the Reformation, by Catholics for the purpose of discrediting Protestantism; and Pascal and Huet, the latter in particular, sought to employ it against 'unbelief.' Huet left behind him, as his legacy to his church and generation, what Mark Pattison has termed 'a work of the most outrageous skepticism'; and Pascal's use of the method has left a standing debate as to whether he himself was a 'skeptic.' In England, on the Protestant side, Bishop Berkeley put forth an argument to the effect that the Newtonian doctrine of fluxions involved the acceptance of unproved 'mysteries,' and that those who applied it had accordingly no excuse for rejecting the mysteries of Christianity.

Finally, it is fair to note that Mr. Balfour's nihilistic treatment of reason has a surprising sanction in Hume, to say nothing of the other writers who have practically limited reasoning to mathematical deduction. That great thinker, with his frequent great carelessness, wrote that

'Our conclusions from experience [of cause and effect] are not founded on reasoning, or any process of the understanding' (Inquiry concerning the Human Understanding, Sect. iv. Part ii., par. 2).

'All inferences from experience are effects of custom, not of reasoning' (Sect. v., par. 3).

'All these [spontaneous feelings] are a species of natural instincts, which no reasoning or process of the thought and understanding is able either to produce or to prevent' (Ib. par. 6).

But Hume, be it noted, would in his earlier life have recoiled from Mr. Balfour's religious Irrationalism, for in his deistic period he wrote that the belief in Deity is 'conformable to sound reason.' And, what is more important, he in effect cancelled his own remarks on reason, above cited, by writing as follows in Note B on the Inquiry cited:—

'Nothing is more usual than for writers, even on moral, political, or physical subjects, to distinguish between reason and experience, and to suppose that these species of argumentation (sic) are entirely different from each other. The former are taken for the mere result of our intellectual faculties, which, by considering a priori the nature of things, and examining the effects that must follow from their operation, establish particular principles of science and philosophy. The latter are supposed to be derived entirely from sense and observation, by which we know what has actually happened from the operation of particular objects, and are thence able to infer what will for the future result from them.... But notwithstanding that this distinction be thus universally received, both in the active and speculative scenes of life, I shall not scruple to pronounce that it is at bottom erroneous, or at least superficial.'

Hume, it will be observed, is not here bent on vindicating the rational character of direct inference from observation: he had set out in the text by disparaging customary thinking as non-rational; and he is now claiming for the 'reasoning' man that experience goes a long way to generate his reasoning processes. 'The truth is,' he says in his final paragraph, 'an inexperienced reasoner could be no reasoner at all, were he absolutely inexperienced.' It is a fragmentary note to a hasty passage; but at least it concedes that reasoning is largely a matter of inference from experience, and thus decisively gainsays the assertion in the text that no inference from experience is an 'effect of reasoning,' inasmuch as it says such inference is reasoning; that reasoning is a working of the mind on the facts of life; and that the common distinction between reasoning and [beliefs derived direct from] experience 'is at bottom erroneous, or at least superficial.' If, he says in the fourth paragraph of the Note, 'If we examine those argumentswhich, in any of the sciences above mentioned, are supposed to be the mere effects of reasoning and reflection, they will be found to terminate at last in some general principle or conclusion for which we can assign no reason but observation and experience.' If an argument be not a process of reasoning, neither word is intelligible. If an argument terminates (=has one end) in a conclusion founded on observation, and if that observation be a 'reason' for a proposition, then arguing is reasoning.

If not, what is Mr. Balfour's book? By his own definition, that is 'outside the sphere of Reason,' inasmuch as it is a series of negative propositions which, like their denied contraries, must be 'incapable of proof.' What term, then, would he apply to his argument, if he admits that he is arguing?

The philosophic skeptic, it would appear, has logically overreached himself—a very usual consummation. There is little sign that any of the religious skeptics above named ever made any converts to religion; and there is much 'reason' to think that they turned many to unbelief. Mr. Balfour from time to time speaks of 'reasonable people' and of 'absurdity.' But he leaves us in the dark as to what absurdity means, and his thesis excludes from the 'reasonable' class alike all religious persons and all scientific persons, unless, possibly, mathematicians as such. Since there is no 'reasonable assurance' for the belief that the sun will rise to-morrow, and politicians have no ground in reason for anything they say as such, the mass of the ordinary beliefs of educated mankind are not reasonable or rational; and since we have no 'reason' for believing in either mortality or immortality, we can have no reason for believing (whether we do or not) in Mr. Balfour, who avowedly believes in both without reason. His book, by implication, is not an appeal to reason, is not a process of reasoning, and can give no 'reasonable assurance' of anything, positive or negative, to anybody. All this by his own showing.

The rationalist, it should seem, has small cause to deprecate such antagonism. He could hardly have a more comprehensive clearing of the field of dialectic for the formulation of his own conception of reason and reasoning, and his own appeal to the reason of reasonable people. As thus:—

1. Reason is our name for (a) the sum of all the judging processes; (b) the act of reflex judgment; (c) 'private judgment' as against obedience to authority; and (d) the state of sanity contrasted with that of insanity; and 'a

reason' is a fact or motive or surmise which we judge sufficient to induce us or others to believe or do (or doubt or not do) something without much or any danger of error, failure, or injury.

2. Reasoning is our name for the process of comparing or stating 'reasons why' certain propositions or judgments should be believed or disbelieved, or certain acts done or not done.

3. We are emphatically 'in the sphere of Reason' when we are reflecting and reasoning, as distinct from merely feeling, sensating, desiring, or hating; but even the feelings are, as it were, part of the stuff of Reason. Strictly speaking, we are in the sphere of Reason even when we believe what we are told to believe on matters outside the knowledge of our instructors (in so far as we credit them with greater wisdom than our own), or try to believe that what we would like to be true must be true because we would like it (inasmuch as we are proceeding reflectively on a 'reason why'); though in these cases we are reasoning fallaciously—that is, in a way which can lead to manifold error and injury.

4. Reasonable is our approbatory epithet for an action, course, or person that is guided by reasoning which we see to exclude most risks of error and injury—save of course where the taking of risk of injury is assumed.

Every one of these definitions is justified by the dictionary to begin with, though the dictionaries, of necessity, note further conflicting meanings, as when reason is indicated as 'the faculty or capacity of the human mind by which it is distinguished from the intelligence of the lower animals,' or hazily distinguished, on philosophic authority, from 'the understanding.' But the lexicographer loyally notes that a reason is 'a thought or consideration offered in support of a determination or an opinion'; and that to reason means, among other things, 'to reach conclusions by a systematic comparison of facts,' 'to examine or discuss by arguments.' These senses are implicit in daily usage.

The concept of Reason, in short, must include the whole factory of beliefs. The judging faculty, the judging propensity, is a complex of instincts, experiences, inferences, and necessities of thought. It originates at an animal stage, and conserves to the last animal elements — as when, without any process of calculation, you infer, as it were through the muscular sense, that a top-heavy omnibus is likely to overbalance, or that in riding your bicycle round a sharp corner you must incline your body inwards. It deals with diet and medicine, art and industry, no less than with theology and science and politics. In the former, its accepted procedure is obviously a set of survivals of more or less tested ideas from among an infinity of detected mistakes; and the moral law of the intellectual life for the rationalist, the principle which best justifies his assumption of that name, is that every belief or preference whatever is fitly to be tried by all or any of the tests by which beliefs have been sifted in the past, or may more effectually be tested in the future. We are to do with both our religion and our science in general what we have done in the past and are still doing with our medicine, our sanitation, our education, our physics, our historiography.

Without more ado, then, we may proceed to ask how reasons for beliefs are ultimately to be appraised by reasonable and consistent people — in other words, how beliefs are honestly to be justified.

7. THE TEST OF TRUTH

It may have been observed, with or without perplexity, that Mr. Balfour specified a 'need for religious truth' as his ground for holding his unspecified 'theological beliefs,' this after bracketing Religion and Science as alike 'unproved systems,' consisting (by implication) of a body of propositions as to which we have not 'any ground for believing them to be even approximately true.' The skeptico-religious conception of truth being thus found to be as nugatory as that of 'reason' put forward from the same quarter, we are compelled to posit one more conformable to common sense, common usage, and common honesty. For the generality of instructed men, truth in secular affairs means not merely 'that which is trowed,' but (a) that which we have adequate 'reason' to trow, and (b) that of which our acceptance is consistent with our way of testing credences of any or all other kinds. The ultimate criterion of our beliefs, in short, is the consistency with which we hold them.

By this test the ground is rapidly cleared of skeptico-religious literature. That puts a spurious problem to mask a real one. The question for us is not and cannot be whether, seeing that by inference from experience some of the beliefs we now hold are likely to be found false by posterity, we have any right to accept one belief and discredit another. The skeptic is himself doing so in this very argument, and all the time. His whole intellectual life is one of judgments and preferences. There is no intellectual life without them. The question is whether we have applied to any one belief or set of beliefs the tests we have applied to others: whether, for instance, we can honestly profess to believe in prayer or the doctrine of the Trinity or heaven and hell as we believe in Gresham's Law or the effects of quinine or the roundness of the earth; whether we have criticised the religion in which we were brought up as we criticise Mohammedanism or any other; whether we have scrutinised the legends of our creed as we have scrutinised the legend of King Arthur and his Knights; or whether, on the other hand, we hold the atomic theory or faith in vaccination by mere authority, while we dispute about religious teaching in the schools.

This does not mean that we are to apply the same kind of test to every kind of proposition; that we are to ask for evidence of immortality as we ask for evidence of the Darwinian theory. The test is one of consistency. Does the belief in immortality, we are to ask, consist with either our knowledge or our imagination? Do we hold it critically and coherently or as a mere congeries of irreconcilable propositions? Do we ask ourselves what we mean by 'meeting again'? Is it anything more than a fantasy which we affirm for our own comfort or the supposed comfort of others, or for the sake of mere conformity with popular sentiment? No thoughtful man, perhaps, will deny that he holds some of his opinions by some such easy tenure; were it only for the reason that consistent ascertainment is often laborious, and that common consent has to be allowed to take its place in regard to many beliefs of plainly inferior importance. But religious beliefs are not so classed by those who seriously debate them; and here, if ever, the challenge to scrutiny and consistency is imperative.

And so disturbing is the challenge that for centuries past the higher religious consciousness has been engaged in an unceasing effort to persuade itself and its antagonists of the secular or mundane reasonableness of its supernaturalist creed. Religious life is seen going on at two widely removed standpoints: one that of the emotional believer who knows no conceptual difficulties, and is concerned only to maintain in himself and others the quasi-ecstatic state of faith; the other that of the would-be reasoner who is concerned to secure peace of mind by arguing down his own misgivings and the positive antagonism of unbelief. Between those extremes, probably, is lived the mass of religious life so-called, untouched either by ecstasy or by conceptual unbelief as distinguished from passive conformity. But the conflict of the thinking minority is unceasing; and orthodox professions of triumph deceive no one who is really engaged in the struggle.

On both sides it has long been a question of balancing 'probabilities,' a conflict of 'reasons.' Bacon, declaring that he would 'rather believe all the fables in the Golden Legend and the Koran than that this universal frame is without a mind,' opened a door that let in all the forces of doubt. The

Koran is the form in which the God-idea recommended itself to the Moslem mind, as the Bible is the form in which it commended itself to the Christian; and if for each the other is always fabulising in detail, where could be the certitude of the common doctrine? Was mind any likelier to be the form of the power of the universe than any other of the anthropomorphic characteristics of Jehovah and Allah and Zeus? However that might be, Bacon was appealing to the sheer sense of probability; the 'Evidences' of Grotius were addressed to the same kind of judgment; and Pascal's 'wager' was a blank appeal to the principle of chances plus the instinct of fear. Butler, anxiously striving to reduce the straggling deistic controversy to its logical bases, accepted the test of probability as the guide of life; and Gladstone, his last champion, with all his show of sheer faith, strenuously endorses the doctrine. The vital question is seen to be, then, whether the Butlerian 'believer' or the rationalist is the more loyal to that standard of probability by which each avowedly guides himself.

But Butler, in the very act of professedly basing his case on probability, introduced the contrary principle. Gladstone, gravely reprehending that Jesuit doctrine misleadingly termed Probabilism—which permits of a choice of the less probable course in morals and belief—supposed himself to be upholding a true Probabilism in Butler. The fact is that Butler, seeking to checkmate the Deists, committed himself to anomaly as a mark of revelation. 'You believe,' he virtually argued, 'in a benevolent God of Nature, though Nature is full of ostensible cruelty and heartlessness: if these moral anomalies do not stagger your deism, why should anomalies in the Scriptures be for you an argument against their being a divine revelation? Should you not rather expect to find difficulties in the revelation as in Nature?' So that the champion of the standard of probability ends by putting an element of improbability as a mark of divine truth.

It was long ago pointed out that Butler's argument was thus as good for Islam or any other religion as for Christianity. Gladstone framed a futile rebuttal to the effect that Christianity had marks of truth, in respect of prophecy and miracles, which Islam lacked—a mere stultification of the

Butlerian thesis. The Moslem could retort that if his creed succeeded more rapidly than the Christian with special marks of anomaly upon it, those were presumably the right anomalies! By the Butlerian analogy of Nature, what sort of anomalies, pray, were to be expected in a divine revelation? Gladstone actually made it a disqualification of Islam that it had succeeded by the sword; this when his own creed had slain more than ever did Islam. But on Butler's principles, his plea was vain even if true. If a divinely ruled Nature be red in tooth and claw, why should not the divine faith be so likewise? What is the lesson, by deistic analogy, of the volcano?

The complete answer to Butler, of course, lies in stating the simple fact that analogy leads rationally to the conclusion that all the alleged revelations are alike human products. If every one in turn is found to embody cosmological delusion, historical falsity, fabulous narrative, barbarous ethic, and irrational sanctions, all of which are by each believer singly admitted to be the normal marks of human stumbling, the case is at an end. The one salient and sovereign probability is the one that the believer ignores.

When this mountainous fact is realised, the full force of the Butlerian argument is seen to recoil on its premiss no less than on its conclusion. The dilemma that was to turn deists into Christians is simply the confutation of all theism. Upon none of the tested principles of inference now normally acted on by men of science, men of business, and men of affairs, is it rationally to be inferred that the universe is ruled by a superhuman Good Male Person, who loves and hates, punishes and rewards, plans and reconsiders, injures and compensates. As little are we entitled to infer that it is governed by a Superhuman Bad Person, or a number of Superhuman Persons, male or female, good or bad, or both. The polytheistic and theistic solutions are the natural ones for unreflecting ignorance and priestly policy, and the latter remains the natural one for reverent ingrained prejudice, alias inculcated faith; but it is only so much sophisticated folklore for the student of life, nature, history, philosophy. The latest forms of it are but defecations of the earlier. For Arnold, trained in reverence and avid of reverend sanctions, the deity of his fellows is confessedly but a 'magnified non-natural man'; and his substituted 'Something-not-ourselves-which-makes-for-righteousness,' in turn, is for his critics but an evasion of the problem of the something-not-ourselves-which-makes-for-unrighteousness.

In sum, then, the case for rationalism as against the creeds is that they recognise no rational test for truth, and apply none. They are all, to say the least, grossly improbable in the light of the fullest human knowledge; and the acceptance of them means either passive disregard of the principle of sufficient reason or the habitual employment of arguments which upon any other kind of issue would be recognised by all competent men as at best utterly inadequate. Theology is the most uncandid of all the current sciences; its results are the most self-contradictory; its premisses the most incoherent. Upon those theologians, then, who accuse the rationalist of self-will and prejudice, he is forced to retort the charge with a double emphasis. They are daily disloyal to the Canon of Consistency, which is for him the moral law of the intellectual life. Claiming to propound the highest truth, they override all the tests by which truth is to be known.

The modern defence of 'faith,' whether Christian or theistic, is less and less an attempt to prove truth of doctrine—save as regards the defence of historicity; more and more an attempt to prove its usefulness or its comfortableness. Faith has turned utilitarian, as regards its apologetics. John Mill erred somewhat, indeed, in endorsing the statement that down to his time much had been written on the truth of religion, and 'little, at least in the way of discussion or controversy, concerning its usefulness.' Christian bishops early learned to claim for their creed a gift of prosperity; and in the eighteenth century there was an abundance of utilitarian vindication of the faith. But latterly this has more and more coloured the whole defence. Either as a promise of peace or as one of comfort and stimulus, as a plea for emotional indulgence or for the joy of the sense of deliverance from responsibility for sin, as a guarantee for good government or as a condition of general progress, Christianity is defended on any ground rather than on that of the truth of its narratives or the conformity of its doctrine to good sense, moral or other. And the pleas are entertainingly internecine.

One day we are told that it makes for race-survival; the next, that it is a spiritual stay for races that are dying out, and a great deathbed comfort to ex-cannibals, with a past of many murders. A creed which involves a cosmology is recommended, not by such arguments as may commend a cosmology, but by pleas of subjective agreeableness which in any discussion of historic fact would be felt to savour of trifling.

And this simple and spontaneous sophistry is in a measure kept in countenance by quasi-philosophies such as that of the 'Will to Believe' and that latterly termed Pragmatism. The former, as brilliantly propounded by the late Professor James, amounts simply to this, that in matters on which there is no good or sufficient evidence either way, we do well to believe what we would like to believe. As the precept comes from the thinker who passed on to students the counsel of Pascal concerning the opiate value of religious practices, it is easy to infer how it will tend to be interpreted. And the second philosophy is like unto the first, in so far as it conveys, under cover of the true formula that the valid beliefs are those which affect action, the antinomian hint that if we think we have found any belief a help to action, it is thereby sufficiently certificated as true.

The rationalist comment on Pragmatism, thus applied, is that it really discredits the religious beliefs of most men, inasmuch as they never relate their faith to action in general, would not stake a shilling on a prayer, have no working faith in providence, and do not in the least desire to pass from this life to another. But these men do not study philosophy; while the emotional believers, who really feel their faith to be a help in life, do not need the pragmatist's precept, and believe without it.

What is true in Pragmatism is of the essence of Rationalism. Our lives at their best are made valid for us by our mutual trust, our reciprocal sincerities; and Rationalism consists in the effort to extend intellectual and moral sincerity to the study of all problems. It may permit, none the less, of some such genial or affectionate glozing of some facts as love and friendship tend to set up in the relations of persons, tolerance taking on the vesture of sympathy; and it no more makes for Gradgrindism, or the belittlement of any of the higher joys, than for concentration on the lower. Its antagonists alternately indict it for 'gloom' and for licence; for coldness and for 'Epicureanism'; for seeking only happiness, and for turning happiness out of doors. The contradictions of the indictment tell of its collective origin in mere hostility of temper. Rationalism, of all codes and modes of life-philosophy, must most seek to make the best of life.

Some professed rationalists, indeed, at times grind in the mills of the Philistines by professing an apprehension lest their fellows, in pursuing truth, should lose sight of beauty; and such misconceiving mentors plead confusedly for some formal association of rationalism with the arts of feeling, with poetry, with music, with drama, with fiction—as if without cultivating these things in the name of Rationalism we should be divested of them or discredited as not possessing them. The fallacy is of a piece with that which identifies Christianity with progress in civilisation. The rationalistic bias is in actual experience found to be as compatible with any æsthetic bias as with the scientific, specially so called; though in point of fact a scientific culture is in itself more conducive to rationalism in respect of historical and ultimate problems than is culture in the arts, which are mostly enjoyed, appraised, and even practised without deliberate resort to critical analysis.

Some rationalists, again, have been found to contend that the critical analysis of things æsthetic is destructive of æsthetic joy—an error of errors, involving blindness to the facts that even a science is in itself ultimately perceptible as an artistic construction, and that all the arts live and renew themselves by the sense of truth. The solution of the verbal conflict lies in recognising that rationalism is after all but a name for considerate consistency in the intellectual life, where consistency is still so sadly little cultivated, and where established habits and institutions tend so powerfully to its exclusion; whereas in the arts there is no call for such specific championship. There the very joy of novelty is soon potent to overcome the resistance of habit—which, for the rest, roots in structural or acquired limitations not greatly dependent upon cultivation or neglect of the rationalistic habit. A man of science or of critical research may be dull to new refinements of æsthesis where an unscientific emotionalist may be sensitive to them.

Recognising all this, the balanced rationalist will shun as a special sin of religion the ritualising of his joys, the sectarian extension of his differences of credence to the field of æsthetics. His rationalism as such implies no one of the special 'isms' of the arts; though there he may be an 'ist' like another. For him all art, all literature, all beauty, is so much of Nature's fruitage; and Christian cathedral and Moslem mosque can yield him pleasures which Christian and Moslem can never derive from his distinctive intellectual work. He may even take artistic satisfaction in contemplating the figure of the winged angel which Christianity took over from Paganism, without believing it to be the image of a reality, as so many pietists have so childishly done for thousands of years. 'Religious' music can minister to him in virtue of the common psychosis. His very names for himself and his intellectual code are but insistences on complete inner loyalty to a moral law which most men profess to obey, and which all of necessity obey in many if not in most matters.

The time is for him even in sight, as it were, when most men will recognise and live by that law; and when that day comes there will be no more need to profess rationalism than to profess, as a creed, any of the daily reciprocities by which society subsists. But till that day comes he marks himself, and is marked — to his frequent discomfort, it may be — by his insistence, in the deepest matters, on that law of truth which so many still persistently subordinate to pleas or preferences of authority or habit, convention or subjective taste. Avowing it as his bias, if so challenged, he claims that it is the bias to perfection in the intellectual life as the bias to order and sympathy is the bias to perfection in the civil.

8. ULTIMATE PROBLEMS

To a surprising degree, the philosophic disputes of the ages turn upon the same problems; and to an extent that is nothing short of sinister, they resolve themselves for most of the onlookers, if not of the participants, into the question of the maintenance of the popular religion. Thus academic theists in our own day are found resenting the tendency of ancient freethinkers to discredit and disestablish the Gods of Olympus, who for the academics themselves, as for everybody else, are a set of chimeras. Are we to infer that the current academic philosophies, even where constructive, are no better bottomed than the popular credences they seek to shelter? Kant's 'critical' philosophy was by himself soon turned to the account of pulpit religion; Fichte ended in restating the gospels in terms of his pantheistic personal equation; Hegel soon attained to the championship of the Prussian State Church; Lotze has reformulated Christianity to the end of giving it continuance as a creed for the educated. Nietzsche said with substantial truth that the vogue of Kant has been that of a philosopher who enabled theological teachers to put a philosophic face upon a doctrine nototherwise presentable to their students; and the vogue of Berkeley in England has been of a similar kind.

In our own day the fortunes of new treatises in popular philosophy turn upon their adaptability to orthodox sophistics. Our generation has seen in succession (1) the absurd work of the late Professor Drummond on 'Natural Law in the Spiritual World' welcomed as turning the tables on 'science' by showing that its doctrines are fundamentally at one with those of the faith; (2) the still more absurd work of Mr. Benjamin Kidd on 'Social Evolution' hailed as demonstrating by ratiocination that the reasonable course for society is not to reason; and (3) the incomparably subtler books of Mr. Balfour acclaimed (whether or not read) as proving that reason cannot bite on religious opinions, and that we could never enjoy our music and our dinners as we do if we thought of ourselves merely as evolved from animal forms, without somewhere inserting Deity as the sanction and exemplar of our preferences, æsthetic or moral. Always the acclamation tells of a passion somehow to humiliate 'science,' to put reason in the wrong, to triumph over 'negation,' to show that there are more things in heaven and earth than are dreamt of in any philosophy which does not make play with 'spirit,' worship, and the supernatural.

The cure, however, is never found to be permanent; and latterly we see the not very accommodating philosophy of M. Bergson grasped at as yielding some kind of weapon wherewith to beat back the advance of the ever-encroaching assailant. Sooth to say, neither the analyses nor the syntheses of M. Bergson are in any way damaging to rationalism, or in any way rationally ancillary to supernaturalism. The anti-rationalists have clutched eagerly at his dictum that reason, considered as a light upon the universe, is a poor thing; and that there is something in us higher than intelligence. Apart from the disparaging form given (gratuitously) to the content of these propositions, there is nothing in them that has not been rationalistically put. That is to say, it is a rationalistic proposition that new truths are reached neither by deduction nor by induction, but by a leap of the judgment, by spontaneous guess or hypothesis. What then?

To say or imply that the guessing faculty is something incomparably higher than intelligence is one of the inconsequences of M. Bergson, whose very acute analysis is apt to play upon special problems without controlling his own dialectic procedure. The sobering fact is that the false hypotheses are reached in the same way as the true, the wrong guesses in the same way as the right, the delusions in the same way as the discoveries. The very theses in science which M. Bergson contemns were reached by the way which he arbitrarily pronounces 'superior' to the way of reason. And the court of appeal that determines which is which, is after all just that intelligence or reason which M. Bergson, imitating one of the old methods he has ably helped to discredit, had verbally belittled in merely discriminating its function. No prerogative whatever can thereby be conferred upon either the guessing faculty or the guesser as such. The 'divining' faculty is not more divine than another: it is not really more wonderful to catch fish than to cook them; and the gift of establishing hypotheses is as rare as the gift of framing them. When all is said, the self-confidence of the transcendentalist avails for none but himself: as his own craving for countenance shows, his hypothesis must pass muster before reason if it is to persuade.

And for this among other reasons, M. Bergson's attack upon Spencer and other generalisers in science for their 'mechanical' way of conceiving evolution is no blow to 'science,' as M. Bergson would probably avow, though he is lax enough to delimit science at times in his dialectic. His own way of stating evolution is only another mode of science. To call 'science' superficial is to be so; for the demonstration that any scientific doctrine is inadequate must itself be science or nothing. And here again M. Bergson's criticism, though searching, is not new, however freshly put. In respect of his sociology in particular, Mr. Spencer has been repeatedly so criticised; and it is here alone that his limitation of method is really serious, inasmuch as it affects his prescriptions. As regards the conception of sub-human evolution, his way of reducing the past to 'pieces' of evolution is not only not injurious, it was the only way in which evolution in Nature could well have been realised by men. M. Bergson is all for the 'creative' aspect of evolution, the Living Now, the emergence of the latest phenomenon as not merely the result of the one before, but the living manifestation of the whole. But this is simply the instinctive, pre-scientific relation to the problem, returned to and restored, as it had need be, to its place in a scientific schema from which it had been dropped precisely because it led nowhere.

M. Bergson has suffered, probably, from the zeal even of instructed exponents, to say nothing of the acclamations of the amateur; but perhaps even M. Bergson, by reason of his linear mode of advance, misconceives the full significance of his own restatements of perceptual and conceptual fact. His theorem has been represented as vindicating the thesis of Mr. Samuel Butler's 'Luck or Cunning'—the thesis, namely, that animal survival and progress are to be conceived in terms of gift or effort rather than of environment; that Lamarckism, once more, is truer than Darwinism. But the argument overlooks the fact that Cunning may be envisaged as Luck; and that Lamarckism without Darwinism halts far worse than Darwinism without Lamarckism. At best, the 'living' view of evolution is but a complement of the other, a return from analysis to outcome. Put singly, it is no addition to knowledge.

'We called the chess-board white: we call it black,'

the onlooker might say, with Browning; while the analyst might retort that, like the savage, he was quite conscious of the ever-moving point of life, the Living Now, but preferred to give his mind to the still and spacious past, and 'to cut it up into pieces' by way of knowing something about the law of things, past, present, and future.

The morally valid element in M. Bergson's insistence on 'creative evolution' (again an old term, by the way) is the vindication of personality as a creative form. But this was not necessary as regards the rational determinist, whose position really assumed it, though possibly individual determinists may have obscured the truth by their phraseology. As of old, anti-rationalists persist in assuming that the determinist view of things, mostly accepted by the rationalist, impairs character by reducing will to a 'mechanism.' But that is a calculated obscuration of the doctrine. It is a bad sophism to assert that 'the rejection of mechanism by non-libertarians is a mere phrase. Sooner or later they have to affirm that man is mechanically determined.' It is not so. 'Going Universe' negates Machine. That concept adheres to the schema of those who affirm the universe to be made: Naturalism excludes it. Theistic determinism does make man a mere vessel, a tool: for Naturalism he is an individuation of the Living All. The intelligent determinist never was and never will be put out by his conceptual recognition of himself as part of an infinite sequence; and he has no need of M. Bergson's (untenable) restatement of the problem of free-will and determinism to the effect that the will is sometimes free and sometimes not. That is indeed a hopeless fallacy—an illicit inference from the unduly stressed re-discovery that new truth is reached by a leap and not by a sequence. To say that we are 'free' when we have an original idea or guess is to miss the logical truth set forth by so unsophisticated a philosopher as Locke—that the concept of 'freedom' is irrelevant to every process of thought. M. Bergson insists on the irrelevance of spatial terms to psychic processes, but overlooks the equal irrelevance of terms of preventable personal action.

Precisely because he is, so to say, the latest outcome of the universe, the rational determinist will insist upon 'pulling his weight' and having things go, as far as may be, in the way he prefers. No one's right is better! And he can confidently claim that here, where he is philosophically at one with the thorough-going theist, he has all the possible moral gain from his determinism without an iota of the theist's perplexity. That gain consists in the lead to mercy in human affairs. The theist-determinist is certainly not, as some Christian rhetoricians (ignorant of Christian history) affirm all determinists must be, either a coward or a licentious knave, in the ordinary sense. Augustine and Luther and Calvin and Knox were neither, though all four were sadly sinful men. But the theistic determinist is open always on the one hand to the paralysing thought that if he should err he is resisting God, and on the other to the equally deadly instigation of the thought that those who resist him are God's enemies. To escape both snares he must turn thorough pantheist=non-theist. And the upshot is that the theistic determinist is never merciful, whereas the rational determinist is at least under a logical compulsion to be so, however he may resist or divagate. He is free to defend himself, and to defend society; but in so far as he hates and hurts he is illogical, and in so far as he makes punishment retaliation, or prevention punitive, he is either confounding himself or setting lust against light.

Were there no other betterment from the substitution of the non-theistic for the theistic relation to ultimate problems, this might be held to outweigh all claims on the other side, to say nothing of the simple rationality of the negative solution. But that is, of course, in itself decisive. The logically strongest form of the theistic case as against the non-theist is that, even as he lives and moves in gravitation without any subjective consciousness of it, so he may be controlled in every thought by a transcendent volition. But this argument, which excludes M. Bergson's formula of our occasional 'freedom' of will, equally shelters determinism from the contention that we are 'conscious' of freedom of thought. Even as we are demonstrably conditioned by gravitation while unconscious of its control, we are demonstrably conditioned by our experience and structure as regards even our guesses. Neither the ignorant nor the ungifted man makes the valid new hypothesis.

There remain for use by the theist only the old reproaches that a non-theistic philosophy is 'desolate,' 'negative,' 'materialistic,' and incapable of explaining the universe. The last is a mere ignoratio elenchi, for the very essence of the non-theistic challenge is that every 'explanation of the universe' is an imposture, exposed as such either by its self-contradictions or by its evasions. The normal theist either bilks the problem of evil by avowing it to be a mystery—a thing he cannot explain—or falls back on the alternative evasions that there cannot be good without evil (that is to say, that good needs evil, which is thus good) or that 'partial ill is universal good,' and that evil is thus non-ens—which again is a denial of any moral problem. To complain of 'negation' as such while making such negations as these is to be more entertaining than impressive.

And to be told that, in putting aside these logomachies, he is depriving himself of intellectual and moral comfort, is for the rationalist no perturbing experience. He is what he is because he knows the utter inanity of the theistic declamation about his putting in place of the 'Immeasurable Divine Eye' a 'vast bottomless Eye-Socket'; knows that for the vast mass of mankind the imagined Eye has been a menace of all their myriad ills, that its levin slays them like flies, that the iron has entered uncounted millions of souls who daily prayed for divine succour. The prate of his 'negation' is as childish as the complaint of the avowal that we cannot reach the planet Jupiter, not to say the constellation Hercules: he does but affirm the incontrovertible truth that an infinite universe cannot be compassed by our thought, and that to assert its permeation by 'mind'—a finite process of perception and discrimination, verbally defined as transcending both—is to pay ourselves with words. To the Berkeleyan formula that existence is only as perceived, and that without perception there can be no existence, he answers, similarly, that the first proposition means only that we perceive what we perceive, and that the second is mere intellectual nullity, a verbal pretence to unthinkable knowledge. The further Zenonian frivolity of the denial of an 'external world' needs from him no further comment than this, that in the terms of the argument 'external' has no meaning, and the proposition, therefore, none either. It may be left to the denier of existence 'outside consciousness' to tell us where consciousness is. The inquiry may perhaps lead him to the discovery that he, the professed foe of materialism, has been limiting consciousness to the compass of the skull.

The ultimate claims of the theist to spiritual superiority and serenity are oddly bracketed with the charges of arrogance and Epicureanism constantly made by him against his antagonist. All alike are irrelevant to the issue of truth; and all alike tell of other motives than those of truth-seeking. Those other motives are substantially what our theological ancestors called 'will-worship,' self-pleasing, the bias of pre-supposition, the aversion to surrender. All theistic dialects alike sing the song of self-esteem. The spiritist pronounces his gainsayer 'impercipient,' thus inexpensively cutting the knot of argument; and, himself a wilful continuator of the thought-forms of the savage, declares himself to be transcending the earthiness of the sciences in virtue of which he is civilised. All this is a poor way of proving serenity; as poor, at bottom, as the perpetual display of wrath at gainsaying by men who claim to have the backing of Omnipotence. Consciousness of intercourse with the supernatural has never ostensibly availed to give the common run of theists imperturbability in their intercourse with the naturalist.

And if in the stress of controversy the rationalist should in turn prove himself capable of perturbation, let him, avowing that he claims no supernatural stay, at least plead that he sets up no intellectual 'colour line,' and that his gospel is after all fraternal enough. Once more, he does but ask the theist to take one more step in a criticism which he has already carried far, with small trouble to himself. Every religion sets aside every other: the rationalist only sets aside one more. Every theist has negated a million Gods save one: the rationalist does but negate the millionth. And in doing this, he is not committing the verbal nullity of saying, There is no God—a formula never fathered by a considerate atheist. God, undefined,$=x$; and we do not say, There is no x. Of the defined God-idea, whichsoever, we demonstrate the untenableness; but in giving the theist an inconceivable universe we surely meet his appetite for the transcendent.

Rationalism, when all is said, is the undertaking, in George Eliot's phrase, to do without opium. And perhaps the shrewdest challenge to it is the denial that the average man can so abstain—a denial which may be backed by the reminder that the framer of the phrase did not. A jurist once cheerfully assured the present writer that the mass of men will never do without alcohol and religion. He was not aware that he was adapting a Byronic blasphemy. It may be that in a world in which most men chronically crave alternately stimulants and narcotics, he was in a measure right. But as one of his two necessaries is already under a widening medical indictment and avoidance, it may be that the other will fare similarly. In any case, is not the ideal a worthy one, as ideals go?

9. IDEALS

Ideals, obviously, are part—the best part—of our bias: to that admission we may unhesitatingly revert. By his bias the rationalist can afford to be tried. Intellectually he makes truth his paramount consideration, and morally he insists upon the same sincerity in things intellectual as men profess to practise in honourable intercourse. I have heard a distinguished Christian scholar denounce these canons as commanding such an outrage as telling a child of its mother's shame. The charge is an illustration of the strange malice of which piety is capable. No human being ever proposed to communicate all truth of any kind to children; and the limit to the gratuitous telling of wounding truth is fixed by normal courtesy and sympathy as regards the sufferings even of adults. The charge is in fact one more illustration of the anti-veridical bias of pietism—the need to distort and pervert the case against the rationalist.

And if pietism can thus distort the bearing of the intellectual canons of rationalism, much more habitually does it distort the specific purport of rationalist morals. The fact that naturalism implies utilitarianism is transformed into the proposition that utilitarianism means the subordination of all play of sympathy to an incessant calculus of profit. As we have seen, theism and Christianity alike do chronically subordinate the veridical instinct—a moral instinct like another—to lower considerations of utility; and only too often in history do we see them annulling the instincts of mercy and reciprocity by the law of dogma. Not by propounders of that test is the rationalist to be put to shame. The very basis of Christianity, in fine, is an other-world utilitarianism. 'What profits it a man——?'

Utilitarianism means for him, in brief, what it meant when it first took shape as a moral plea—the testing of traditional moral canons, and their annulment when they are seen to be mere survivals of barbarism, sanctioned only by custom and religion; never the substitution of a calculus of utility for an accepted moral canon in every act of life. Any general moral rule rationally seen to be broadly utilitarian is thereby vindicated qua rule; and to put its practice at the hazard of every trying emergency would be to sin against the very principle of utility. For the rest, the rationalist has his moral bias like another; and in virtue of it, as animating rationalisers of various developments, has been wrought the main part of the modern purification of working morality, though the moral instinct in religious men has responded, and has at times initiated reformation. It is left to the religionist to argue that a bias which has wrought for truth, justice, and mercy will somehow fail to preserve other virtues. No reminiscence of the sexual history of Christian societies can restrain Christian advocates from imputing to the spirit of reason a tendency to promote promiscuity in the sex relation and thus to overthrow 'the family.' Holding as they do that the family is the keystone of society and civilisation, they in effect argue that the practice of rational calculation of means and ends will destroy both. Pessimism could no further go; and if this be not the height of pessimism it is a stress of false-witness which puts the accuser outside the pale of controversy. As an imputation upon known rationalists in general the theorem is simply false. The systematic revival of Aryan polygamy has been a religious process; and the freest practitioners of sexual choice among reasoning unbelievers, the Russian Nihilists, have been notoriously monogynous.

It may be hoped that we shall in future hear less and less in these matters of the extremities of orthodox malice or misgiving, as we hear less and less of the old plea that whereas a bad believer may be held in moral check by his religious fears, a bad unbeliever will fear only the police. The statistics of the jails do not encourage that line of apologetics; and the records of the Society for the Prevention of Cruelty to Children do not go to show either that rationalism makes parents cruel or that religion keeps them kind. The plain truth is that upon bad bias law is the main check; and that the most vaunted religious methods of developing the good bias of the weak have latterly been systematically supplemented, in the organisation, for instance, of the Salvation Army so called, by secular methods which are the avowal of the final and general futility of the others.

In no other direction are the moral ideals of rationalism less fully vindicated by the movement of civilisation. The humane and scientific treatment of criminals has actually been antagonised, in the name of the

Christian doctrine of sin, from the ranks of the Howard Society, established to promote such humane treatment. Rationalism can no other: religion seems willing to leave it the credit. Above all, the great cause of Peace on earth—the very motto (a mistranslation, as it happens) cited as that of nascent Christianity—visibly depends more and more on the spread of rational calculation, the spirit of reason, rather than on that of faith, however faithfully many a good Christian continues to plead for it. There is no Peace Church: even Quakerism has latterly had its war-mongers; and there is no record in history that the doctrine of the Fatherhood of God ever withheld men from fratricidal war.

We shall still hear, it may be, that the intellectual pride of rationalism is in tendency anti-democratic; Gibbon and Hume being cited as cases in point. And the rationalist democrat, shunning the lead of his antagonist to panacea-mongering, may here at once—or once more—confess that the spirit of reason in things intellectual is no guarantee for the immediate elimination of egoism in human relations. Christianity has claimed to be such a guarantee—with the results we know. But it is flatly inconceivable that the spirit which challenges all authority and anomaly in doctrine can tend to conserve either tyranny or social and political inequality. The very apologists who make the charge are the successors and coadjutors of those who have charged upon irreligious philosophy the generating of the French Revolution. Anti-democratic rationalists there will be, as there have been; but for every one such there are a hundred of the contrary ideal; and it is not in conservative parties that they are found to avow themselves. For rationalism, on the side of thought, must forever mean liberty, equality, fraternity, 'the giving and receiving of reasons,' the complete reciprocity of judgment. To all races, all castes, it makes the same appeal, being as universalist as science, naming no master, proffering no ritual, holding out no threat. The rationalist, as such, can have no part in the errant Darwinism which would conserve struggle because struggle has yielded progress; much less in the pseudo-Darwinism which would further degrade backward races because they have been ill-placed. Of race-hatred he cannot be guilty without infidelity to his first principles.

And if all this be termed vaunting, the objector may, perhaps, be placated by the repeated avowal that neither is rationalism proclaimed to be a wholly new way for the nations, nor is the rationalist as such acclaimed as the monopolist of good. He respectfully urges upon the best and ablest followers of other flags that under his they will not deteriorate or be less cherished; that their gifts are precious in his eyes; that he wants their collaboration for humanity's sake. His panegyric of Reason is but the praise of what is wisest and best in man: his 'ism' is the concern to put off dead husks of opinion, to lift all life to the plane of light. The religionist may, if he must, come over with permission to call the cultus of truth and sanity a religion: some there are who suppose themselves to solve the dispute by that means, as Spencer thought to solve it by inviting Science and Religion to join hands in an avowal of a common ignorance. Such eirenicons do not seem widely acceptable: it is really better to let words keep their historic meanings than wilfully to change their values.

But if the question be whether rationalism is a creed to live by, an ideal to live by, let these pages be taken as giving part of the answer.